ALL OF THE RHYMES AND TIMES OF Dorothy Elaine

ELAINE SHARSHON

To order additional copies of this book, contact:
Xlibris
844-714-8691
www.Xlibris.com
Orders@Xlibris.com

ISBN: Softcover   978-1-6641-3439-3
         EBook   978-1-6641-3438-6

Print information available on the last page

Rev. date: 10/08/2020

DEDICATED TO MY CHILDREN, CATHY
CAREN, LAURIE AND BOBBY.

ABOUT THE AUTHOR

Creating a thought is like baking a cake... it either rises to the occasion or falls flat in the middle of it, I've never been much of a baker, but I like to think my musings are tasteful.

Dorothy Elaine

CHILDREN

Oh wither the woman so tired and worn, I feign I've yet to meet,
Who can truly say she hasn't thrilled to the patter of little feet.
God lends a child for a little while, to raise, to guide and to love
And sometimes 'ere our task is done, they return to him above.
They're certain to bring us some sorrow, but the joys are so hard to beat,
For everyone listens with rapture, to the patter of little feet.

Written in 1948 to cheer myself up after having three children in 16 months

A TELEPHONE OPERATORS JOB

It's not that I don't like my job, indeed I really do
But I would like to gather facts and pass them on to you.
Now we're the voices with a smile and must be so polite
Our personalities are worn thin till we get home at night.
There's many different kind of folks that we must cater to,
And so that you will understand, I'll mention just a few.
There's the nervous man who answers with three very loud hellos
Some wrestle with their phone as tho it were the deadliest of foes
Then you have the timid soul, with voice so soft and meek,
He hems and haws and stutters before he starts to speak.
And the man who to never seems to know exactly what he's after,
Or the character whose heard a joke, and fills your ear with laughter
Then there's the man who acts as tho he's known you all his life
You know he want an outside line, so he can call his wife .
Now you know a hundred voices, and with each voice a name,
And then someday you meet the man, but somehow it's not the same.
You soon forget how tall he was, if he was nice or clever,
But let him hang up in your ear, you'll remember him forever.
We're sometimes tired and out of sorts but this they can not see
For we just smile and hold our tongue until we close the key.
So now you know the story of the daily job I *do*
But making it a pleasant one, always depends on you.

Written in 1942 while working at Consolidated Vulttee Aircraft corp.

LITTLE BOYS

I think that I will never find. a wonder like a small boys mind
A mind on year round mischief bent, with energy that's never spent.
With kites and worms and tricks and toys, are filled the minds of little boys.
A boy who may in summer be, a Tarzan swinging from a tree,
To bless our lives with extra joys, is why God gave us little boys.

Sing this to your little lad to the tune of "trees"

THE GOLFER

He walks about on velvet green, and hears the serenading thrush
And now and then the rivulets soft giggle thru her maddening rush.
Trees nod approval of the day, beneath their cloud flecked canopy
How can this man, midst beauty such, so acerb and ill tempered be?

My husband was an avid golfer, but was never satisfied with his game

SATURDAY SHOPPING

Over the hill to the market I'm trudging my weary way
Over the hill to the market and oh what a list today!
Now Dotty says she would gladly go, except for the children three,
So I go trudging back and forth, but a shopper I'll never be.
She'll tell me of bargains in this and that, there's an art to buying a roast,
When my only ability lies in, getting least for the most.
I can test all the bread for freshness, squeeze grapefruit to see if they're ripe,
Compare brands and priced till sundown, and still the lady will gripe.
The roast is too small or too fatty, the wrong kind of juice, she'll say,
And yet I go trudging on and on, while Dottie at home will stay.

TWICE BLESSED

Why is it parents always have a tendency to boast
How extras special their child is, of brains she has the most.
They'll give a recitation how she never gets in trouble
Braggarts beware, I've got you beat because I'm bragging double
My oldest girl's the essence of what makes a small girl sweet,
Then looking at the youngest, she's a double, just repeat.
Their attitude, their character, their faces both the same,
With golden hair and dimpled cheek, their beauty I proclaim.
We have our mother daughter talks, all very seriously
Oh what a thrill with four big eyes just sparkling up at me.
When now and then we go to town the girls find it a bore,
With people asking "are they twins?" in each department store.
They tease their teachers, and exchange their proper seat in school,
In different beds at bedtime, they, their mother try to fool.
And when at night they're tucked away, and I sit down to rest.
I feel the right to doubly brag, because I'm doubly blessed.

BIRTHDAYS

My mind is a muddle of doll carts and rings of
Tea sets and dresses, all little girl things.
The time's growing short, I must make up my mind
I've just a few days, a present to find.
I try, but in vain, to recall if at eight,
My most beloved toy was a doll or a skate.
A little girl's watch! Ah now that's just the
Thing that a grown up feeling and pleasure will
bring. My, what a relief, a decision at last.
it's always a blessing when birthdays are past.
Now do I relax? Not this side of heaven! In just a
few months my son will be seven.

twins 8th birthday 1954

THE FISHING TRIP

We packed the children neatly in among the rods and reels
Then started out with all the hope the novice fisher feels
Then on the way we gave advise on how it should be done,
From where and why and how to cast, to don't get too much sun.
And then we told them stories of the fishes we had caught.
Their length, their breadth, their monstrous size, the savage battles fought.
Till finally we reached our spot, by fisher's instinct led,
with Hip length boots, with bait and hooks, the grown ups forged ahead,
Oh never to have made that trip must be my life long wish,
For though we did the bragging the children caught the fish.

Written after a trip to the mountains

MATING TIME

GARDENING

My friends are planting gardens, and all expect to see
The sprouts come up and flowers bloom, all excepting me.
I watch them work with envy, and see their gardens grow
Daisies, phlox,and pansies, all neatly row on row.
Last year I got to tinkering and as I sowed grass seed,
The rain came down in torrents, leaving naught but weed.
I planted some petunias, the easiest flower to raise,
But somehow they never got beyond the budding stage.
So now they're planting gardens, and oh so proud they'll be
All gazing at heir work, well done, all excepting me.

As the children grew so did my outside interests, but not necessarily my talent

THAT FEELING

I've known the pangs of hunger, and the thirst of sheer desire,
I've felt the pangs of jealously consume me like a fire
There isn't an emotion, with which I haven't met
Fear, sorrow, grief and loneliness, I've known them all, and yet,
A feeling comes upon me, and seeps into my soul,
Scourges into my consciousness just like a burning coal.
A different kind of feeling from all I've ever known,
A tightening of the stomach, a chilling to the bone
It turns my knees to rubber and makes me gasp air,
All these are my sensations while in the dentist chair.

Written after a wisdom tooth extraction

TO A ONE TIME FRIEND

Folks likes and dislikes differ, their judgments not the same,
And from these controversial facts, they've improvised a game
To play, a statement is required, plus a friend who disagrees
And then the fatal question, "Would you care wager please?"
Now I loathe a man who gambles, tho I know the thrill he gets,
But neath a man who gambles lies a man who doesn't pay his debts.

NECESSARY EQUIPMENT

A watch. A knife A piece of string, a safety pin or two
A one time rusty door knob, all polished up like new,
A water pistol, fireworks, a tiny cardboard rocket,
These things were all discovered in a small boy's left hip pocket.

My son was a collector as a very young man

TODAY (WRITTEN IN 1954)

The different phrases young folks use, I guess are mostly to amuse
But just imagine what would be, if all were taken seriously.
Just as the saying "he became a bookworm" has acquired fame
Thus all the people reading books would somehow alter in their looks.
The person sometimes called a square,would find it hard a hat to wear.
And then the girl "sharp as a tack" all femininity would lack.
Now folks have called me a "good skate", and yet I can't appreciate
This younger generations talk, tho not alone at this I balk.
Their baggy clothes, a hot rod car,. And bebop sets my nerves ajar,
But times must change, or so I'm told, I guess I must be getting old.

Written in fear of the teenage years

MID-LIFE PREGNANCY

This life of ours is so complex, and sometimes most confusing
With incidents that bend the heart and mind, not any way amusing.
To understand just how it is misfortune comes to you,
An honest upright person in all you say and do.
The tossing of the dice they say, the falling of the chips,
Your wheel of fortune spinning, but these are only quips.
I say there is a plan for us, a universal one
A plan that's set in motion from the day our lives begun.
And things that start out poorly can oft times turn out fine,
Improving, as the years go by, like the aging of old wine
So step right up and take your blows written on today's life's page
And trust that someday they become the joy of your old age.

The middle name of my mid life child is Joy

FIRST GRANDSON

Our little Kyle was born into a family of girls
So all we knew was frilly cloths and making perfect curls.
But as he grew he taught us that boy's aren't always mean,
And made us come and watch him when he joined the Little League Team.
He loved to watch the weather man, and ventured into art,
It seemed he always had the edge, because he was so smart.
Then all too soon he sprouted up and was on his own.
In Farragut Military school so very far from home.
Today he flies for US Air and still does all he can
While the ladies of the family proudly watch the family's only man.

First and only grandson

LIFE

This world of ours is filled with fears,
With heartache, sorrow, worry, tears
So difficult seems the labyrinth to cross,
That in it's turbulence we toss,
Blind to the joys and lost in despair
We find our life is barren and bare.
Some look back on days gone by,
And reminiscing evokes a sigh,
Then some there are that think that they
Were never blessed with a happy day.
So let the dead past bury it's dead,
Plan for your future, look straight ahead
Lift up your face to the sun and you'll see
Twas lover's of life we were all meant to be.

Written while suffering with
"empty nest syndrome"

SOLILIOQUY ON DEATH

A chasm in the darkest night
Suffused with suffocating dark
Completely destitute of light,
Impervious to one small spark
Midst vastness beyond comprehense
All ostentatious pomp has flown
There, a soul awaits it's fate,
Despaired of comfort, save it's own.
Will some congruous loneliness
Then come and take rein of it's heart
Or fear, to rend the mind and soul apart?
Can this then be the ultimate,
This oracle of black and gloom
And desperation knowing now,
There's no return beyond the tomb.

JEALOUSY

She tapped first lightly at my heart
A fool, I let her in
Her kiss of venom stung my brain.
And steeped my life in sin.
Tenacious company was she,
Covetous of my soul.
A parasite, fed by my thoughts
My brain. devoured whole.
I, void of her intrusion
She ruled without a ban,
Her scepter now becoming,
The lewd heart of a man.

Written for a friend who lost his wife because of his jealous nature

22

AN OIL PAINTING DONE WITH A KNIFE, NO BRUSHES

BENEATH A WILLOW TREE

A mass of trembling fantasies, like lacework, delicately sewn
A pattern made intricate, articulating on it's own.
Designed with natural elegance, so lithe, and more than beauteous,
That man made imitations seem stupid and most 'ludicrous.
A hallowed spot, magnificent, a shrine with lace like canopy,
Pray let these maudlin bones of mine, make their perpetual rest neath thee.

Dedicated to my favorite tree in Trexler Park

THE COMING OF FALL

I've never really cared for fall, despite it's wondrous leaves,
To me it marks the spot in time when all of nature grieves
When everything turns gray and dull and shrubs of green and rust
Desert the trees and then become discolored piles of dust.
When all the world gets dimmer and birds sing lesser songs
When the days grow ever shorter and the nights are dark and long
When the rays of sun seem fainter, and the winds begin to moan
Lamenting all the pleasures of a summer that has flown
But there is nothing to be done, but simply wait till when,
At last, the world returns to life, and spring rolls round again

WINTER IN THE NORTH

I cringe beneath my blanket in the murky morning gloom,
Afraid to guess the temperature within the chilly room,
Intrepidly I place my feet upon a floor of ice
Which prompts sweet thoughts of summer,
When the world was warm an nice.
Huddling in my furry robe I rush downstairs to see
The timer on the coffee pot has once more failed me.
I sit and wait impatiently while trying to remember
The warm sun's rays,the grass. the flowers. Egad it's just November!

HOLIDAY BEHAVIOR

How 'oft I've heard the thought proclaimed, until it's most worn thin
Since Christmas comes but once a year, how lucky we've all been.
Between preparing for the feast, with Christmas gifts to buy.
The mothers find themselves worn out till Christmas time is nigh.
The bank account, especially, is always in distress,
And yet each Christmas we spend more instead of spending less.
But I wonder if you've noticed this, which somehow compensates,
How Billy's hung his hat and coat, and Jane's replaced her skates,
How Tommy's washed his hands and face, not needing to be told
Somehow it seems their manners have improved a hundred fold.
Alas it lasts a few short weeks, it's very plain to see
That only before Christmas, kids are good as they can be.
And so I sit and ponder, which evil is the worst,
The draining of the patience or the draining of the purse.

CHRISTMAS 2005

Twas the night before Christmas and Santa was pissed.
He couldn't believe the length of his list,
This new generation just seems to need more
Making demand unheard of ever before.
Time was when a doll or a football would do
But now they're looking for that wonderful new
Computer with printer and scanner to boot,
An I Pod, a cell phone, and clothing to suit,
A ring a watch and a few new CDs.
A digital camera surely would please .
The elves are all weary, the reindeer distraught,
It's plan today's children have never been taught
That givings a pleasure that money can't buy,
Let's hope by next Christmas they give it a try.

Today's grand children

MY GARDEN KINGDOM

Each night when darkness, like a girth. entwines itself about the earth,
Like king Midas I sit and see my wealth reveal itself to me.
My chair, by moonlight, turns to gold, I sit upon it Monarch bold
It's golden gleam, no beauty bars, but stands reflected in the stars.
Sweet zephyrs, alien to storm, make sighing trees my minstrel form,
Contented dynast. as the hours. turn dewdrops diamonds on my flowers.
A wondrous kingdom, all my own, I'd barter for no other throne.

Like a good bottle of wine, I improved with age
as far as gardening is concerned.

MUSINGS ON TURNING 80

When I was young I dreamed a lot ' bout what I'd want to be
An artist or a writer, would I take up chemistry?
Would I try my hand at stardom, and trod the stage a Queen?
Become the greatest actress the world had ever seen.
Would I foster some great program, and discover something new?
Would I gain the recognition bestowed on very few?
But as the years unfolded, it was very plain to see,
That I was just the marrying type, so I raised a family.
And tho I've never known acclaim or starred on old Broadway
My heart and mind still tell me I've surely had my day,
Surrounded by the ones I love, and those who all love me
The role of mom and grand mom, was a part just made for me.
Now as the years roll on me I look around and know,
That fame is very fleeting, but love can only grow.
So here I stand, without awards, no Oscars at my side,
My trophies, my sweet memories of family and my pride.

AMERICA

God bless this wondrous land of ours, with all it's splendid things
It''s rolling hills, bright city lights, and the freedom that it brings.
It's safe to speak or worship, to stay at home or roam
To the shores of the Atlantic to the frigidness of Nome.
We all can run for president, or sit back and criticize,
We can read a book or burn a book. We're the master of our lives.
So get down on your knees at night, and give thanks to God each day.
For you were blessed by being born in the good old USA.

Written after WWII,when it was still politically correct to be a patriot

90TH BIRTHDAY

Well here I am in my old age
My book of life on it's last page
The years have flown by, oh so fast
All filled with memories of the past.
Yet somehow very deep inside
There lurks a valley deep and wide
Where all my youthful thoughts still hide
Where friends were many and foes were few,
And every day was bright and new,
Where life was easy and sort of slow
But warm and lit by love's sweet glow,
It's where I long always to be
Because it's more the REAL me.
My face may wrinkle, my feet may swell,
My mind create a constant whirl,
But inside still lives that little girl.

A PAINTING OF SHELLS WAS DONE DURING MY LOVE AFFAIR
WITH SHELLS PERIOD IN THE SEVENTIES.

FLORIDA AT IT'S BEST

THE ROAD OF LIFE RUNS MUCH SMOOTHER
WHEN YOU SHIFT INTO
IAMBIC PENTAMETER!!

THE REMAINDER OF THIS BOOK WILL BE DEDICATED TO
ALL MY THOUGHTS AND POETRY AFTERR THE AGE OF NINETY.
I HAVE TRIED DESPARTETLY TO MAINTAIN A SENSE OF HUMOR
NO MATTER WHAT LIFE THREW AT ME. I CREDIT THAT
ALONG WITH A FEW GIN MARTINIS FOR THE BOLSTERING
OF MY SPIRITS, MY HAPPY OUTLOOK ON LIFE AND MOST
CERTAINLY MY LONGEVITY.

My wonderful room mate for the last twelve years. She is also a writer.

A PURRFECT LIFE

By Cally, the Cat

My name is Cally, and I'm a twelve year old female tortoiseshell female who had led a life you may be interested in reading about. I truly don't like to meow about myself, but my owner tells me I'm exceedingly smart, and if there's anything I don't like, it's confrontation. So I just agree with her. When I was only five months old, my first owner abandoned me to the S.P.C.A because of allergies. This really tweaked my whiskers because she really had not had me long enough to make the determination that it was me. Then along came my present owner who was clever enough to see immediately that she had chosen well. My new mistress had just lost her husband, so I became the fur ball of her life despite my constant shedding.

All went well for about three months, when suddenly she decided she could not live with a litter box in her house, and I became the target of toilet training. By now she had already taught me to sit, stand on my hind legs only, give a high five, and jump through a hoop. Being a normal kitty I did not take well to the idea of all that water so close to my dainty little paws, and so began the six month saga of animal resistance versus human resolution. I finally succumbed to the praise, petting and delicious treats surrounding me when I did my duty. My only regret was that she wouldn't teach me to flush because she was afraid I would run up her water bill, using the toilet handle as a new toy.

As a reward for her goodness to me, I cry when she comes home at night so she thinks I missed her, sit on her lap when she watches TV, and sleep in her bed at night so she's not lonely. In return I let her brush me every day, cut my nails once a month and allow petting whenever she feels lovey. No wonder cats have nine lives, we work so hard to deserve them.

CLOUDS

Have you ever lain on soft green grass and gazed up at the sky?
Have you seen the great formations on the clouds as they pass by?
I once saw Mr. Lincoln with top hat, beard and all
It seemed I saw his face quite well, but could not see how tall.
At sunset I see flowers but I've never seen a tree,
Just once I saw a country, it was the boot of Italy.
I think the month of May is best to get the perfect view
The sky is usually always clear and wears it's azure blue.
Imagination plays a part in each and every sighting,
Mine runs rampart most the time, accounting for my writing
Just get a lawn chair and prepare to get an emanation,
Then just relax and wait a while enjoying the sensation.

WHISHFUL THIKING

I wish that I were young again, tween seventy and eighty.
I'd spend my life just just having fun and shed the things too weighty
I'd make my life a Ferris wheel with ups and downs, but thrilling,
Then find some zany friends to help me make it all fulfilling.
We'd go to different places we have never been before,
Spurred on by curiosity we'd enter every door.
Discovering things we've heard about, but never thought to see.
And realizing happiness, is life's most precious key.
A trip like this would surely call for many, many things,
Your best attire, your pinching pumps,your pearls and diamond rings.
And what about your makeup,and cremes for neck and face?
Your rollers scents, and curling iron are deserving of some space.
A gown's a must to sit beside the Captain at his dinner.
A cover up for swimming. I've not gotten one inch slimmer.
Now as I think it over, my life's never been a bore
I've been to many places and opened many a door.
This world today is sometimes more than this old heart can stand.
My coffee must be decaf my meals must be bland.
But I should be contented with memories from the past
And more than merely grateful, they were good enough to last
So I am satisfied to sit, to wait to watch, and see
If you enjoy your golden years quite as much as me.

DECISIONS, DECISIONS

Remember that old tune from World War 1, Oh How I Hate To Get Up In The Morning? I, for one, am definitely in tune with that tune. I'm no scientist but am most aware of the speed of light getting here too early in the morning. The body is totally adverse to ingesting any foreign substance before 10:A.M. I can't quite recall where I got that information but if memory serves me, as it usually does, I do believe it was in a Medical Journal many years ago, As a matter of fact, now that my mind is is in a state of deep perusal I do remember an-mother tidbit of value. Sleeping in adds to longevity. I consider myself a perfect example of that truism. I must find that article and read it again. Also, you early risers, just remember that God made sunsets for those of us who miss out on the morning show. Anon other important decision in this life is is whether to shower in the morning or in thee evening. My personal preference is most positively evening, after my body has been subjected to all manner of things, invisible to the naked eye. I think I read, in that same Journal where, if you could see all the microscopic organisms that have set up housekeeping all over your torso during the space of one day it would settle the question of the time best to bathe. I love getting into my Lysol sprayed clean bed after my antibacterial soap shower, then cuddling up with my cat. Cally. So now to the biggest and most fun decision you'll ever have to make, but not without it's die hard backers on each side. Whether it is nobler to hang the toilet paper with the paper ejecting from the top or from the bottom of the roll. Men never have to deal with this, when thy run out they simply retrieve a new one and set it on the closest vanity or tub. When these monumental crisis rear their ugly heads, it is most usually the little woman who will come up with the final solution. By this time perhaps you don't really care about my comfort station so I will simply say if you were to thread a roll through the bottom, and add two eyes you would end up looking at the Pillsbury dough boy with this tongue hanging out. Decisions, Decisions!!!

THE SEXES

In my search for a topic for this month I at first decided to discuss men.. This thought lasted for only the few seconds it took me to remember the subject has has been discussed ad infinitude. Everyone knows that even at birth, and through the toddler stage they are already attracted to and cry to be with a beautiful women, mom. Their high school years all their ambition is spent on trying to become a jock and watching pretty girls. By college they have graduated to cramming and chasing pretty girls. By thirty they marry a pretty girl and give up ogling for a year or two, but in that interim, they are miraculously transformed into couch loving, beer drinking fanatics who devote themselves to the red zone every Saturday, Sunday, Monday and, Thursday. contenting themselves with the sight of cheerleaders and bellowing obscenities when their team loses the ball This conception was so well embedded in the minds of America that in 2014 a brave publisher began a new magazine entitled, The Good Man Project. This was an an effort to alter the impressions of insensitive, dead beat, absent, and wife beating guys into hard working, respected providers, who love and care about their families. Good Luck!

I may as well continue down this avenue, and blab about women, because that's what women do best, blab. If you ever have the need to broadcast an event, tell one woman and add the words, it's a secret We love being the first to know and can't help ourselves. when it comes to propagating the news. We love to gossip and take incessant enjoyment noticing what our friends are wearing and complementing them. We should give up the negative asides we are sometimes guilty of making once they are out of earshot. A man would never discuss another man's clothing. Women are lacking in self esteem,especially if they had a brother. Boys, for whatever reason, seem to be doted on in families. They become a hero in Little League, we play with dolls. We want to be pretty and admired, so we shop at the Bob Ton and frequent the beauty parlor. Why is it men look so good in a dusty tee shirt, chin stubble and a Mohawk? Women are emotional because they are filled with frustrating maternal love, over which they have no control, and can not suppress the need to spread it everywhere on every one they know and love. Men find any public show of affection an embarrassment and most unmanly. Women are whiny and sometimes need solace and comfort, particularly if it's about money. the children, in laws, or any situation affecting them simultaneously. The males interpretation of this is nagging, and fills the husband with resentment, which, most often, turns into brawling. Making up is great they say, but once the format is drawn it can easily become habit. . A woman is crafted, by God to be forever forgiving .. I can't imagine any sin a man could commit that his wife (because of family) would never forgive. (Look at Hillary) With the opposite sex, not so. Men are owners, don't mess with their property. unless you are totally prepared for endless retribution. It would seem most of the foibles of women have been compounded by the inconsideration forced on them by men.

I love writing totally unbiased articles. It's like watching Fox News. or CNN. I believe I have thoroughly delved into the human race. Maybe next time I'll write about other animals.

WORDS

I have spent a lot of time lately thinking about the word, WORD. and what happens to it when you merely add an adjective . There are good words, bad words meaningless words, words of wisdom, hurtful words, useful words, useless words, descriptive words, short and long words. I could go on forever but my mind has been dwelling on how and when this phenomenon began. How did man first learn to speak? Was it a bad a curse word because some caveman burnt his finger on his first found fire? Perhaps a chimp, hanging from a treetop bellowing for a mate, and meeting with success. This, of course taught the other primates how it's done and they all learned to say "Hi Babe," in chimpanzee. Again, it could have all started with sign language, and gestures. Some people still talk with their hands. Just watch Beth O'Rourke. Adam and Eve spoke Hebrew, supported by the fact he named her Isha, according to Genesis. That name only has meaning in Hebrew. Wonder how she slipped the word, apple in there. I also wonder what happened in The Tower Of Babel when everyone began to speak in different tongues. I would think the tumult was very similar to the sounds that emanate from Palm's dining rooms at dinner hour. Some linguists believe that the origin of the spoken word dates back ten thousand years, and started in Africa. Here I always thought everything started in California.

The experts also proclaim the ability to speak sets us apart from all other animals. This type of analogy is hard for me to handle. My cat, Callie, understands every syllable I utter in her direction, including her name. I, in turn, can decipher the exact meaning of her many meows even better than I can understand people who mumble. Some of her demands are so distinct you would have to be a dog not to understand them. Speaking of dogs I have seen many different breeds that can say the words I love you better than most men. They suffer through lonesomeness, caring, devotion, and heartache the very same way humans do, with the ability and brain power, to convey their feelings to their masters. Those masters, by the way most definitely come in second when it comes to the brain department. Animals save humans, humans take animals to the ASPCA.

I'm getting maudlin, which Webster says is an unhealthy interest in unpleasant things. So I will end my article with happy words. frivolous, comical, ludicrous, side splitting laughable, uproarious, funny, hilarious and stinky feet.

SOUNDS OR NOISE

There I was sitting down at my kitchen table, pondering the worlds problems, particularly the new virus and its many challenges, while I waited patiently for the ding of the toaster oven announcing the readiness of my breakfast bread. My microwave was already relentlessly beeping, demanding I remove my heated cup of coffee. Before I could do so, my medical alert button began urgently announcing I had failed to recharge it the previous evening. When all the sounds quieted down I prepared myself to enjoy a leisurely breakfast, but it was not meant to be. The moment I sat down, my cell phone blared Hallelujah, Hallelujah, a ringtone selected by yours truly. My decision not to answer, but to continued eating, was a poor one, which subjected me to a small tingling noise, indicating a left message. By the time I pressed my napkin against my snarling lips, I had reached this conclusions. The reason older persons who must wear hearing aids or have the beginning of dementia owe it all to the noises they have been subjected to most of their lives. There was always a bawling baby, boomboxes, blaring horns, bombs bursting in air, shrieking tires, sweepers, sonic booms, and the most destructive of all, the sound of sirens. From birth to our declining years we have been bombarded with noise. Our eardrums and brains have been battered by the electronic age of beeps, bops, binges and baloney. I feel our hearing apparatus and minds are the most overused parts of us,except, of course, for our mouths.

I long for the sounds made by the darling cuckoo clock, or those great chimes emanating from the ancient grandfathers clock, the beauty of the old time doorbells, the bedlam of the circus, a hand pushed lawnmower's click click, the mournful sound of a far away train, the clang of a trolley.

I think that's enough sounding off from me for the moment.

MERRY MONTH OF MARCH

Now enters the month of March created by all the folks who are Irish and all the folks who wish they were. During Pisces I always change my name to O'Sharshon which makes me feel more in touch with the O'Briens the O'Boyles. O'Donnells, O'Connells, O'Connors, O'Dells and oh well I think you've gotten he gist of it by now. I would like to take it one step further, however, to explain, the O stands for "descendant," while the Mac in McCormick. McCarthy. McBride, Mac Dougal. Mac Gowem, MasGinley, and MacQuire translates into "son of "..

In defense of the Irish Catholic propensity toward consuming hard liquor on a daily basis I refer you to the fact that they suffered for 700 years from continuous occupation, religious persecution, intermittent abuse of military colonial rule. These humiliations drove them to the point where every second cottage had its own still, which could produce up to 12 gallons of Irish whiskey at one time. Sounds like something to be admired to me.! It was also expected, from birth, most Irish men were to lead a life which would guarantee their arrival in heaven. No wonder so many became priests. It was a sure way to get on the express . What pressure! By the time the potato blight ended in 1852, many migrated to North America, where they became invisible in America's melting pot and never did increase their self image. It has been written that all of the above has resulted an inferior complex in Irish Catholics which identify as cultural shame characterized by fear. suppressed rage, self loathing and isolation from the community. Makes you wonder how the Jews have maintained their sobriety doesn't it?

Regardless of their vulnerability to booze, just the word Irish brings a smile to everyone's lips . They are a fun-loving, kind, and friendly people, with much to be proud of, their music alone is most memorable. Who could ever forget the song Danny Boy or Molly Malone? Then there's the more than memorable Drunken Lullabies by David King. The Emerald Isle has stupendous rainbows where leprechauns are allowed to keep watch on the pots of gold hidden at their ends, resting on the most fabulous green colored grass existing in our world . The entire male population all look forward to the day when they might meet a kind fairy, who will dust them with Pixie juice, and enable them to fly. (remember Peter Pan.) Those unfortunate enough not to find one, by the end of the day, most likely have concocted their own mode of flying high anyway

They firmly believe in elves and the wailing of banshees who warn of an impending death in a family. I don't believe even a Nazi could have stood up under this kind of harassment, abuse and supernatural superstitions that has been fostered upon the Irish. To tell you the truth, I've had to have a few snorts myself just writing about it. Always be kind to the Irish!!

THE GLORIES OF SPRING

Ah glorious Springtime, my heart flutters like birds
Tongue tied by it's beauty, devoid of all words
For who in this world could sufficiently tell
Of the beauty of roses and do it quite well?
The bloom of the crocus, the tall daffodil,
The pansy, the peony creeping over the hill.
Hydrangea, the beautiful, magnificent in size
The number and marvel of wee fire flies
The dewdrops, like diamonds, shimmer and shine
While crickets chirp happily most of the time
Trees seem more stately, as they stretch to the sky.
The insects sound louder as they buzz on by.
Our orb in the heavens appears so much brighter
Our woes and misgivings so much lighter
My heart knows it's meaning can be only one thing,
The glorious, glorious coming of Spring

OH GLORIOUS SPRING!

I thrill each year to the arrival of Spring
And all of the glories only it seems to bring
The wee little crocus, the tall daffodil,
Roses, tied to the trellis, so stately and still,
The pansies the peonies share their colors with all
And the gorgeous hydrangea will last until fall
The primrose display is a sight to behold
While the field of wild daisies add yellow and gold
The trees and the grasses become startling green
A green that decidedly adds to the scene ..
Then there's the dogwood, magnolia too.
The plum and the cherry, to mention a a few.
I love this time of flowering clover,
And sating myself till the season is over

MARCH

For a moment let us consider the word MARCH in all of it's diversity. The ides of March, the winds of March, the March of time, a Sousa March, the March of dimes, a March hare, March madness, forward March, March on, and of course the month of March, The very sound of the word forces me to realize two months of 2019 have already passed on, and it's time to assess how or if I've wasted them. I finished a painting, read three books and gained eight pounds. Not to say I expected to perform some great feat, but gaining that much weight was most certainly not on my list of things to do. Number one, it is a hazard to your heath, heart wise, and a shock to your system when you accidentally catch your image in the full length hall mirror. Moreover, as you age, all body parts, of their own volition, seem to sink southward without the help of an additional roll or two. When you find it necessary to lie flat on your back in bed in order to successfully zipper up your jeans, consider it a message from Mother Nature, "enough is enough." I speak now from experience. Since turning forty, suffering through diet after diet, and purchasing all available guaranteed to work wrinkle cremes, now cramming my medicine cabinet, has been the bane of my existence. Not once did I even achieve a glimmer of hope that I might succeed, but hope springs eternal in the human breast, and I am no exception. Finally I came to the realization that I remained wrinkled, and now fat. Being optimistic by nature I decided all was not in vain because of the two discoveries I did make, which I'll pass on to you, along with my personal guarantee that they work, They are the two PS, and require both will power and money, so gear up for the secrets of youth. Plastic surgery, and Pushing away from the table. I, for one, am about to diligently apply myself to the later while telling myself how good it is for me, but I do so look forward to desert every night, so if you see me lumbering around the halls, please muter something derogatory. Hopefully my vanity will come to the fore enough to make me a bit more stanch in regard to my diet, and somehow find a way to diminish my appetite . Just think of all the snickering good fun you could have while you, my friends, not only perform a service, but perform your good deed for the day.

AN APRIL FOOL

I would like to take this occasion to report on my diet, but unfortunately, with honesty, there is zero to report. I, however, am not discouraged because although I have failed the first time, I'm glad not to be a skydiver. On that weak attempt at humor I must admit I feel that having a great sense of humor is the essence of a good personality. I'm sure you have all noticed. when making a particularly clever comment. the reactions of the listeners, and how they differ. The man with the funny bone can barely control his belly from bouncing up and down with every twitter of enjoyment, while others slap their thighs and smile in appreciation. The remainder don some sort of weak expression hovering somewhere between nausea and constipation. Life is a gift, that's why it's called the present. given us to enjoy, and it's almost sinful not to appreciate the humor in living it. I feel compelled now to ramble on with intelligent cliches and sayings offered up by today's humorists. and humorless. They are directed to the world, at large, nothing personnel. "You wouldn't be so worried about what people think about you if you realized they seldom do ." A conscience is what hurts when all of your other parts feel good." "A clear conscience is usually a sign of a bad memory." Or a"Good memory is usually the sign of a clear conscience. "Friendship is when people know all about you and like you anyway" Since only 30 days hath April, I feel perhaps I should shorten my dissertation this month, and give other folks a chance to add to April's foolishness.

MOTHERS

Why is it we have so loved our mother
Above our father sister or even a brother?
She's honored each year by all of society,
A day set aside when she's the priority
My mom taught me things I needed to learn
Through patience, and kindness, and her deep concern.
When I did something wrong, which was once the case,
She stood there beside me and shared my disgrace
The first one to praise me when I did something right.
The last one to kiss me and tell me goodnight.
And when something happened that made me feel down.
Shed chided me saying, wrinkles start with a frown.
These wonderful things are the thing all mothers do,
`Because most of f their lives are centered on you
Their love is endless, their devotion sublime.
Their demeanor towards us, almost devise
Praise be to our mothers, the true makers of men,
The goodness we've garnered we owe all to them.

SONG TITLES STORY

Once long ago I ran into a NATURE BOY named Richard who I knew was looking for THAT OLD BLACK MAGIC because, sighing he said to me I CAN'T BEGIN TO TELL YOU… IT'S BEEN A LONG LONG TIME since Billy Bob and I have had any CHICKERY CHICK we don't know whether to become RIDERS IN THE SKY or go CRUISING DOWN THE RIVER to look for some. I told him I'd get ON THE ATCHISON, TOPECK AND THE SANTA FE or THE CHATTANOOGA CHOO CHOO and give the south a try I heard that TENNESSEE had many a PRETTY WOMAN wearing BUTTONS AND BOWS and drinking RUM AND COCA COLA. He then confided they had found two gals in KALAMAZOO, namely TANGERINE and MARIA ELENA and for a while it was like GOING ON A SENTIMENTAL JOURNEY but it didn't take long to discover one was A PISTOL PACKING MAMA and the other, just A PAPER DOLL. YOU'LL NEVER KNOW he said, and I CAN'T BEGIN TO TELL YOU about our HEARTACHES and why I'm not sure I want to be TAKING A CHANCE ON LOVE. We were PRISONERS OF LOVE, and OH WHAT IT SEEMED TO BE, but, TO EACH HIS OWN, and I personally feel like I'LL NEVER SMILE AGAIN, I have such BLUES IN THE NIGHT and wondering if THERE ARE SUCH THINGS as true love. I, being sympathetic to his plight, replied, you need to tell yourself I WILL SURVIVE and if you want to keep STAYIN' ALIVE then find yourself a new girl with PERSONALITY, a DANCING QUEEN, one that gives you NIGHT FEVER. Then take her to a SLEEPY LAGOON, fill her with MOONLIGHT COCKTAILS perhaps buy her a STRING OF PEARLS while whispering softly in her ear, YOU LIGHT UP MY LIFE, LET'S STAY TOGETHER, I JUST WANT TO BE YOUR EVERYTHING, because YOU'RE KILLING ME SOFTLY. I guarantee she'll think she's on a STAIRWAY TO HEAVEN. but If she should answer, I WANT TO HOLD YOUR HAND, reply honey I'M A BELIEVER, I got GOOD VIBRATIONS and I really feel IT'S NOW OR NEVER. Honey, I WANT YOU TO BE MY GIRL

And LOVE ME TENDER. Then buy her one more drink and head for the HOTEL CALIFORNIA, and I'm sure, she'll be the first to OPEN THE DOOR. RICHARD.

LIFE IN THE 6TH MONTH

June. The month of brides and graduates, Flag Day, Father's Day, President's Day, and on Friday the twenty first at eleven forty five A.M. in the Western Hemisphere it will be the beginning of the summer solstice. June is also the month with the longest days of the year.

Lots of things to celebrate and more hours for celebrating them. Statistically, it is the month most weddings take place and there's and old saying which claims, "When you marry in June you're a bride forever." I hesitate to include the assassination of Ferdinand and his wife, which occurred in June and perpetuated the beginning of World War I. I'm not quite sure this has any relativity to the subject at hand.

Moving on to the classy grads. There they are. all decked out in their caps and gowns ready to take on the world and solve it's many problems. Sixty nine percent of these sterling young folks will attend college, but forty percent will drop out before they a complete a four year course. Since fiction is always more interesting than facts. let us suppose that ALL the attendees finish the courses in their chosen field. We would be glutted with educated people and an insufficient amount of positions to accommodate them....... Sorry, must return to facts. Forty per cent of college students do not go into their chosen field the first year after graduating,and many never do. Another dilemma solved by the power of the press in it's never ending recitation of polls, facts, and numbers that only the Rain man could digest. In any event, I consider June one of the months most pleasant in the calendar year because of it's non-excessive temperatures in either direction. In, just a few weeks you'll be sweating your, I don't have to tell your what off, so enjoy June!!

THE GLORIES OF SUMMER

Summer is here, and ain't it grand
The sun washed beaches, the golden sand
Seas of turquoise, green and blue,
All of the things that pleasure you.
Like scuba, snorkeling, surfing waves,
Collecting special shells to save
Amazing sunsets, every night
Till stars shine down their twinkling light.
Palms sway softly, and hum their tune
Till dawn arrives and hides the moon.
Ah, summer, natures gift sublime
Why can't it stay here all the time?

ROMANCE

Romance is the closest thing I know to the game of chess. In the game of "getting to know you," one of the parties is mandated to make the first move. In chess the initial move sometimes dictates the tenor of the entire game. first moves are usually made by pawns, but the trick is to use different pieces and different moves to your advantage, while keeping the other player interested but unsure of his status. You ladies know exactly what I'm talking about. it's known as womanly wiles

As we move down the board now, we must keep intent on securing a safe position for ourselves so as not to make a wrong move, and place ourselves in a precarious position. in the game of "how do i truly feel about this person, all action should become wary and carefully thought out so no one is in danger of hurt feelings, many chess pieces and positive opinions have been exchanged to date, and both games are being taken seriously by now. The person who seemingly has the upper hand can almost feel the thrill of victory, and secretly fantasizes about how his partner will handle the agony of defeat, yet all know and keep reminding themselves how, an unwittingly committed a blunder, brought on by the pressure of the ever closer end of the contest, instantly alters the outcome. while the lovers can be turned into an unrelenting downward spin al by merely using a poor choice of words . no one really feels supreme confidence at this point. as we've all been told, it's not over till it's over.

It's almost unbelievable how these two games are parallel because in the end three are mated if the romance escapade turns out well, Only one out of four turns out to be a loser, and if the losing player is a die hard chessman, he will, most certainly, look at this as a positive experience, and a a lesson on how to avoid the trap he suffered today. resolving never to make the same mistake again, His ardor for the game remains totally undiminished. the winner, however, will be bursting out of his vest thrilled. to the utmost. and, of course, laud his win over his opponent for at least the next two times they meet. the lovers both look at themselves and each other as winners, and holding hands, like Cinderella and her prince fade into the sunset. Checkmate!!

IS IT A BIRD? IS IT A PLANE? NO, IT'S SUPERMOM!!

Mark Twain once announced after just revealing his birth date, "and I remember it as though it were yesterday." I don't believe anyone else, with honesty, could make that claim, but I do believe that every mother in the world could give a second by second description of the birth of her first born. Most babies are born already protesting their entry into this valley of tears, which continues through three months of colic, diaper rash, and just plain crankiness. While moms are usually busy kissing heinies, walking floors, and patting popos, dads are noticeably absent, with the need to nurse their allergies against runny noses vomit and the odor of jarred baby food. Credit where credit is due, they do get involved when the child shows it's first interest in a ball. When a mother really wants to bond with her child, she breast feeds, an act which so pleases the child, he never wants to give it up. There are some downsides for mom resulting from this sacrifice. One is the inconvenience of being a 24 hour a day soda fountain, to say nothing of the poor response from her body to the constant tugging in the wrong direction. In no time at all, baby takes it's first step, and mother is so excited she almost need her own diaper.

Enter the terrible twos. I call this stage the breakage, bawling and bondage age. Baby is determined to break Aunt Millie's antique vase, mom is dead set against this. Baby cries constantly while breaking other insignificant pieces and mom is held captive to keep an eye on her little angel Then, midst many tantrums, tears and cajoling her darling is off to kinder garden. The very first separation between mother and child. Mother waves a tearful goodbye as she watches her sweetie pie kick the seat in front of him on the bus. The kid actually loves school but loves the attention and the extra candy that accompanies complaining even more. Mother is again saddened by the fact that her child's demeanor has changed remarkably since he has been subjected to all those naughty kids in school. By the time said child reaches junior high, mom begins to wonder if she has raised a leader or a follower. High school, at last and we're back to angelic status. Her graduate stands tall, diploma in hand, and has already made plans for college. It's all been worth it, despite the loss of a great figure, and who cares about a few gray hairs anyway? All mothers are, at some point faced with empty nest syndrome. She dons her tear bag once again and wonders how she is ever going to survive life without strife. Enter dad,her hero, who takes her on the trip they were never able to afford before, and she finds herself living a second honeymoon. Within a year mom and dad have settled into their old time relationship, when it was just the two of them. Both afraid to think about what would happen if one of the kids decided to come home. Men intuitively know when to come to the fore.

As I peruse this article I wonder if you may be thinking I am anti-child . Not so! I love and am devoted to all my children. As a matter of fact, when my first delivery was a set of twins, I immediately shifted into overdote. It has only been lately, since I have been scrutinizing the behavior of my great grandchildren, that I have begun to wonder about the rearing of today's child. At the market the other day I was unfortunate enough to hear a mother thank her child for doing what she had asked him to do. I have never once felt gratitude toward any of my children for obeying me, but have patted many a behind for disobedience.

The relationship between a mother and her child is almost unfathomable. The child, knowing in it's heart of hearts, it will never be loved to this degree again in this lifetime, and the mother incapable of not providing it. God most certainly has endowed women with a very special gift. I leave you moms with just one word of warning:

A daughter's a daughter all of her life, A son is a son 'till he takes a wife.

GETTING UP THERE

If I were asked to describe old age I would have to say it is the state of being sick and tired of being sick and tired, but grateful for our longevity. Just living through all the transformation that have taken place during our lifetime are almost beyond belief, along with what we see when we comb what hair we have left.. Each bout of illness is a dreaded and fearful thing robbing us of more strength with every bout. However, looking on the bright side, I have discovered I no longer worry about inconsequential things things that in my younger days would have driven me to distraction.. These days i write my name in the dust on my tables instead of scurrying for a dust cloth before it even settles. I must also admit I do not decorate my bed with it's spread these days, unless I'm expecting company. truth be told, i don't even mind getting back into a totally unmade bed,which in days of yore would almost have amounted to a cardinal sin. Making and having money was the main focus in life when you had a family. Now your family having a sufficient income is most desirable in the event you hit a snag along the line. Funny how we've changed places with our offspring. They are now the ones advising us as to what is best for our own good. They have suddenly gained the wisdom of the Oracle of Delphi and have no compunction about sharing it. I try hard to remember out I can't recall being quite as dictatorial. I console myself with the knowledge all their intentions are dictated by love and then I do whatever I want to.

I have found life to be exciting at any age, and I for one will be sorry to leave this valley of tears, but when I do it will be the same as when I came into it. My only possession, a diaper.

WAIT AND SEE

There was a time when almost every one would use the phrase, "let's just wait and see."Today you wait and wait. Telephone service is a prime example. Just getting to speak to a real live person is usually a minimum of five minutes, and I love the way they keep telling me how important my call is to them, and to please keep holding. I think it's designed to inflate my ego, and it works, I keep holding. How-ever when I finally get connected to the wrong party my bubble bursts because this means they were paying no attention at all to my request.

I find this kind of treatment is prevalent in doctor and dentist's offices. You are courteous enough to accept an appointment made at a time convenient for THEM and they are dis respectful enough to always be late. If we are a no show we are penalized a visit fee. When they are late, I feel we should, at the very least, receive a discount on our bill, which would be determined by the minutes wasted by us, and the worth of OUR time. This is almost as hopeless as trying to get congress to do their job. If everybody I know wasn't on a walker, I'd organize a march on Washington for term limits.

To add further to the disappointments of the day Fed-Ex no longer gives as much as a tap on the door to alert you to the fact there's a package on your doorstep trying to survive the Florida heat. I'll never be able to order Omaha Steaks again. The United States Postal Service is another thorn in my side. Having recently moved, I have been subjected to every possible blunder they could have performed in a move within the same city,(not even a zip code change.) I must report that there was definitely no snow,rain, heat, or gloom of night, to stay these couriers from their appointed path, well, maybe a little heat.

Many centuries ago the ancients wrote that tide nor time waits for no man, but we are a waiting society! We wait to deposit or withdraw our own money from banks that appear reluctant to return it, especially if it's a large amount. We wait for our food in restaurants or a drive through . We wait to get a seat in the cinema, and then wait in line to use their facilities. We watch weather reports before we make outdoor plans

We wait until we receive our income tax refund before we buy that new car we've been looking at all year. We wait for the time to be right before we get engaged, married, or have children. I must admit I have never been mathematically inclined, but I do believe we spend at least one quarter of our lives waiting. Someone once said "what goes around comes around,"so I'll just have to wait and see if things improve as the next generation takes over...That is one of the most frightening things I've ever thought or written.

WOMEN AT WORK

I've just begun to realize that I have worked a lot
It all began when I was born and even when a tot
I had to cry and carry on just to get a bottle
And then to please the family, I had to learn to toddle
I suffered through some diaper rash not uttering a peep,
Because I was considerate of other people's sleep.
And then I went to school to be the first one in my class.
It would not be acceptable if I were not to pass
On leaving elementary school I was voted Queen of May,
My father once admitted It was his proudest day.
By the time I got to High School I found it to be a bore
My grades were suffering a lot and I was suffering more.
Then cane the war releasing all to do what they must do
To save our precious colors of red, and white and blue.
The women worked in factories, the men went off to war
We didn't mind we loved our land and would have given more.
When it was finally over, we married and had kids
But jobs were very hard to find, and kept under special lids
There were no houses either, and looking was a chore.
So we moved in with the in laws, alas, another war.
Time went on the kids grew up, but what a different life
War had taught the women they could work and still be a decent wife.
And so I worked like all the rest, till I was sixty two
Then I moved to Florida and had nothing much to do.
Despite my age I found a job like the one I had enjoyed
Thrilled to death, though slightly worn, I was once again employed
I stuck it out for ten long years, and always did my best
Till my husband said emphatically, it was time to take a rest.
So now I am retired, and sort of glad to be,
But I think I'd take another job if it were offered me.

THE HAPPIEST DAY OF THE YEAR

Christmas, that joyous time of the year, when everybody feels like jingling a bell or two, or perhaps excising their vocal chords with carolers on the corner. The entire world seems filled with love, and new found friends. Whether we're digging in the sand or shoveling in the snow, our good will covers the miles between us, and we rejoice together.

By Christmas Eve the children are ecstatic with anticipatory fatigue and the parents are exhausted and broke. It seems to me those easy assemble instructions for toys were dreamed up by someone with the minimum of a degree in engineering. However, nothing can dim the excitement of Christmas morning. Just the oohing and aahing over the unexpected, and well thought out gifts create an appreciation for one another between extended families, while the aromas of delicacies, not entertained since last Christmas permeate the house. nudging our appetites and delighting grandma, master chief.

It is the one unchanging day in our lives. Most of us have celebrated the traditional holiday from our entrance into history. Mistletoe began being used in Greece during wedding ceremonies many centuries ago. It was thought the plant had an association with fertility. Christmas trees began in the 16th century by devout Germans. The legend of Santa got its start in 280 AD by a monk named St. Nicholas. The practice of gift giving began because of the three wise men's gifts to the Christ Child

However it started, it seems the world is a better place because of it, and the feelings it generates in all of us. Cease fires are ordered, friends and families are   closer, traveling miles to share the day, greetings of good cheer entwine themselves around a smiling world, Prayers are said for peace, and there is ultimate joy because of the heartfelt good wishes and appreciation we feel, and are felt by those we love.

Happy Holidays and Bunches of Mistletoe To All!!

NEW YEAR

We'll here we are again, at the beginning of a new year, with all the past years resolutions still in tow. It would seem we always end the proceeding year armed with strong resolutions, and an endless need to change our ways, which somehow melt away before the first snow fall. I, for one, have come up with five ideas that may make me a better person, and enhance my life at the same time. Number one is stop trying to please everybody., mainly because it is an impossibility We all want to be loved, but a simple compliment, or a sincere show of appreciation for a small favor, will reward you with massive strides toward gaining new and good friends, without all the hassle of a lot of pretense. You'll be amazed at the ease with which you develop a glib tongue. This all reverts back to the days when you could snow your parents and teachers without a second thought. I think it may be genetic.

Number two is to stop living in the past. There is so much regret and would have, could have,should have, in one's life, it's enough to suffocate the word WILL. There is nothing to be gained reminiscing about past poor decision making, or decisions never made at all. The present is the only thing, possible to change, and you have the rest of your life to refine your erroneous ways or continue on the wishful thinking path while you develop a new past you'll soon have to commiserate over. . Do something you've never tried before, be creative, be brave, inventive. Put a stop gap on the old days and delve into the new with vigor and anticipation. Never grow a wishbone where a backbone should be.

Which brings us automatically to number three, putting yourself down. This has become almost a universal past time. We are all vain enough to assume everything that happens is because of us. Not so! I can recall many an event that would have occurred with or without my presence, and others that happened despite it, and still others, because of it. Don't belabor yourself with undue praise, but most certainly take credit, where and when it's due, and don't be afraid to be proud of it. Remember always that you are unique, one of a kind and nothing in this world equals what you are. Even twins are not totally identical. You are a one and only, treat yourself like it.

All of the above are automatically and intrinsically tied to number four which concerns overthinking. the bane of most people's existence, so why do we allow it to plaque us? Very few folks ever make a spare of the moment decision, and when they do, they regret it through eternity. When presented with a dire dilemma or the simplest of decisions, it seems we fall.

into a frenzy of thinking, panicking with the fear of arriving at the wrong determination, Of course many times, once we have found the resolution, we then decide against it at the last possible moment.

Decision making and determination are merits worth practicing. Remember, you only live once, but if you do it right, once is enough.

Number five relates to all of mankind, it is the nature of the beast, Don't fear change. We all do it everyday, but have no control over it. The really frightening things are like, moving, marrying, divorcing, etc. Most of these transformations are resolved with the passage of time, and your acceptance of your new life status. Acceptance is the most important word in the dictionary, meaning according to Webster, acknowledge and approval. If all of us could just be more accepting, we wouldn't be sitting here dredging up new resolutions. Now let me sum up all our magnificent changes for 2019 .We are definitely through with living in the past, and trying to, please the whole world, at large. We will be aware that every day is an opportunity to innovate our lives. We will not fear any kind of change, get a new do perhaps, a snazzier ward robe, a hair color change, grow a mustache, don a saucy chapeau. You may like the way you look, especially if people notice and admire. If it all flops, don't berate yourself, and don't loose that smile, the genuine one, that has endeared you to all your new friends. Last but not least, getting down on yourself produces frowns, frowns produce wrinkles, which, in turn, produce low esteem, forcing us to loose all our good intentions, and it's not quite February/

I now live at the Royal Palms, an assisted living establishment, where I write for the monthly newsletter and enjoy the company of my peers who have brought me to the realization that age is only a number.

THE PERFECT MAN

I saw him standing tall and svelte
Invoking feelings long unfelt.
He was distinguished, debonair
With thick and gorgeous silver hair
My staring finally caught his eye.
He smiled at me, I thought I'd die.
He slowly came across the room,
My heart just knew, 'twas love in bloom.
He bowed to me and took my hand,
As if each sequence had been planned.
His eyes were blue as summer skies,
His lips… You knew, could tell no lies.
He whisked me round the dancing floor,
How could I ever went for more?
He smiled at me with teeth so bright
I almost cried with pure delight
And finally when his lips met mine,
It felt much more than just sublime.
Then suddenly I felt a poke,
And knew that it was all a joke.
My Callie cat had come to bed
And knocked that dream right out my head.

BETER NOW OR BETTER THEN?

Having survived now for almost a century I sometimes find myself pondering the ever pressing question of what part of my life was the best, the most productive the happiest, the worst. Is there a part I'd want to change, a part I'd want to relive or part I'd want to cut out? It always starts out the same way, with comparisons. As a child I loved running through the fields, finding a small stream and submerging my head into it for sparkling drink of freshwater. Now I buy it by the bottle at the market. I'd loved the fresh smell of the outdoors that permeated the house, as I folded the laundry after it whitened in the sunshine. I dryer makes the towels softer. I sterilized and cleaned my kids diapers by boiling them on the stove in a huge vat. My grandchildren's go out with the garbage. I truly loved huddling around the radio with my parents and brothers after dinner to listen to Lowell Thomas with the news, the Amos and Andy show Fibber McGee and Molly, to say nothing of the Saturday night hit parade with "Old Blue Eyes. I was never good at math, but thankful that I had 10 fingers to help me figure out math. Today the need is the same 10 fingers to push numbers into the computer or calculator to get the answer. I never drove a car until I was married and had children, and have never had an accident. My children got their driver's license at 16 and had their first of many accidents by 17. I remember being astonished the first time I heard an airplane actually soaring overhead. Today's skies are crowded with planes like migrating birds, all searching their own destination

All the above, in truth, are nothing but comparisons of convenience. Which was better for me, to have knobby knees and know the pains of the hunger or to be addicted to Mc Dees and be obese? What about love? Was it better to have one soulmate for ever or scout around a bit, since variety is the spice of life? Should I have taken that great job in a different state and relocated, or remained in my position for security reasons and great perks. Life, it seems, is filled with decisions and the phrase quote "if on a I could have a chance to do that over again"escapes everybody's lips at one time or another. Having lived through the depression and World War II I feel grateful for the experience of not getting everything I wanted, and not always everything I needed. It made me strong, independent, frugal, and a part of The Greatest Generation.

Having said all that, my hope for the future is that, if there is something like reincarnation, I want to come back as a dark-haired beauty, (I've always hated having freckles) something along the lines of Hettie Lamar, with a sumptuous body that will guarantee me a very high paying modeling job, so I can travel the world first class, outfitted in nothing but the finest attire. I would prefer to remain SINGLE AND CHILDLESS, 70, (looking like 30 because of plastic surgery) At that point I would consider a companion who never mentions the M word and totally appreciates our relationship. I know you think I'm being very picky, but remember he's getting a wealthy beauty to sport on his arm and you know how older men love that. I feel all my requests are within reason, but perhaps have been somewhat influenced and altered by the ownership of an iPod, PC, a 40 inch flat TV and a cell phone. Did I remember to mention he can't be over 50?

ONE OF LIFE'S DISSAPPOINTMENTS

I write this article as a person who has unwittingly stumbled through life under a vast and long-lasting misconception. From my earliest teenage years I have been taught to perform every act with utmost grace and sterling behavior. I remember, with clarity, the donning of pure white gloves, the bevy of daisies hiding on my broad brimmed straw hat, shiny patent leather, too tight, high-heeled shoes and lastly, the garter belt. This contraption was designed to control and keep all things in their proper position, including the sexy hosiery of the day, which appeared to be manufactured with a mind of its own when it came to a straight line. Most of these articles were high maintenance. The gloves, for example, required daily care to keep them sparkling white, while the straw hats needed to be perched at the exact correct angle to accent our best features, while protecting us from the dangerous rays from Ole Sol We were forced regardless of our meager allowances to purchase our own corn plasters and bunion aids to protect our tortured toes from more agony after stuffing them into ill fitting shoes in order to gain an inch in height and portray dainty steps. In truth it actually was pain that invented women's sexy, swaying walk (watch at the models.) Our feet could no longer stand the anguish and began transmitting messages to the brain to never again allow the full body weight to reach the very bottom of the body again. This could be the reason for so many bad backs.(think about it). The stockings and garter belts were last in the long list of necessities, and as I recall required arduous long periods of adjustments. Many wiggles tugs and squirming were necessary before all the equipment finally settled into its preordained spot. In our small town. every Saturday night and Sunday afternoon young ladies strutted their stuff and young men responded by driving up and down the main street voicing their approval with loud whistles, horn blowing, grunts and all the others sounds male animals make when trying to impress a female. By evenings and, after much eyelash batting and flirty smiling, we had long forgotten our misplaced seams and unseemly slant to our bonnets. We were ready for bed, bath, and Sinatra on the radio. Some of my older girlfriends actually took a spin around the block when they were invited into a boys car. THOSE WERE THE DAYS! WE WERE SO WILD!!

Once I got married and had children, I persisted on passing on all the niceties I had been subject to as a child. How much of it was observed and put to use I'm not sure, but there was for me, enjoyment in the teaching of it. I continue to try to always look somewhat presentable, never to be seen with rollers in my hair, or a towel around my head. I continue to saunter around as if the whole world were watching. What a shock it was to find out no one was watching, or even cared.

During my never ending quest to remain fit to be seen, I developed a sore earlobe from a cheap, but beautiful pair of earrings, and have been trying, through daily medication to nurse it back to its normalcy. At any rate, after puttering with this obstinate lobe and its refusal to be penetrated, for more than 20 minutes, I opted for wearing just one. I thought it might be fun and afford me a little snicker to see how observant older people really are. Surprisingly, after going through two crowded meals, a trip to the manned front desk for needed information, and a game of cards with the sharks at the Palms I came to the conclusion you are all in need of a more diligent ophthalmologist . Once older people's begin the feeding process their interest focuses totally on their digestion system. It's either that or like Rhett Butler once said to Scarlet, "FRANKLY, DOROTHY ELAINE, WE DON'T GIVE A DAM!" Just remember folks, I know where you live.

WHAT TO DO? THAT IS THE QUESTION

I have been trying, for the last several months, to stimulate my brain enough to discover some magnificent something I might do to have a super last hurrah before I go to my great reward. I have always wanted to take a ride in the gas balloon, but the fact that going higher than the third rung on the ladder makes my knees knock and my palms grow clammy, has deterred my leanings in that direction.

Going on safari has a grand adventurous sound to it, but after the kidnapping of Kimberly Sue Endicott, I am bound by common sense to forgo the experience. My bank account could never cover the ransom. Moreover my skin is so thin (and sweet, I might add) at this stage, I feel incapable of surviving a prolonged infestation of insects. However I did discover, while doing my research on the continent there are over 1500 species of insects in Africa. Many of these bugs are edible and filled with more protein than beef or chicken, This fact brings high prices on African markets. Mopane worms go for $85 a million They are excellent for your health along with beatles grasshoppers crickets to say nothing about worms and bees. Maybe if I were to learn to bite back I could live through it and make money.

Lastly, and this one really excites me is as follows; I have been envisioning my bedroom with huge painted murals of Venice on the walls, it's magnificent ancient buildings rising out of the water, each creating its own majestic reflections, a bridge spanning the ceiling overhead, a few docking posts supporting an exotic bird or two, and finally a handsome gondolier gently poleing in the glistening stream at the foot of my bed. It all sounds like a great plan to me. The only hitch to this scenario is, I never want to have to live with my children, so the word eviction has a very negative connotation for me, and stresses me out to the point of obliterating that particular dream.

Now that I have written and reread this article I find myself feeling kind of guilty and ungrateful. I already live on the fifth floor, high enough for me. I have my Cally cat who's more fun than any barrel of monkeys I can think of, and doesn't attract bugs, just eats them. So I guess I'll just drag out a new canvas, some paint and brushes, and try depicting a canal to hang in some auspicious location. Just realized I'm lucky enough to already be living my last hurrah and loving it.

THE ARRIVAL OF 2020

Here we are already in the second month of the new year with out having assessed our fortunes or failures during 2019. First of all did we get more gifts than we gave during the holidays ? Did we take more back then we kept? How much weight did we gain or lose? Was the stock market your friend or foe?. Did the new friends we made eventually fill the void left by the ones we lost? In other words, did the last 365 days end up being a win, loss, or draw?

Now for the personal beauty and well-being department. Will we have to bump up the number of times we spring for a dye job, permanent, or wash and set or just succumb to wearing a wig which covers all deficiencies simultaneously...gray hair lack of hair, fuzzy hair, limp hair, etc. including any holes in your head. When we looked in the mirror New Year's Eve all gussied up with spiffy clothes and grandma's best antique jewelry, did the image smiling back at us still have the same twinkling eyes? Perhaps a few new wrinkles, despite the drawer full of cremes and guaranteed blemish removers brought a tear to your eye drowning out the twinkle. Then there's those little ugly brown marks that seemed to adorn your body overnight. How cruel it was for someone to name them old age spots, liver spots, or senile freckles. Don't forget to check your height for shrinkage, and while you're at it, try to discern whether or not your face is closer to the ground from walking a bit more bent over than in 2019.? Have you had to say goodbye to any of your favorite molars forcing you to change which side of your mouth you must now use to chew? Has your sight dimmed at all or can you still read the telephone book? How about those two appendages at the end of your legs? Any new corns or bunions? How about feet fungus?

If any of your answers to the above questions contain a large number of yeses, just remember to look at the optimistic side of your situation. You are a year older and still looking at the green side, in addition you're very lucky to be living at the Royal Palms were when you begin your tales of tribulation, your listener nods an understanding head, and allows you to wallow in your misery while they cope with their own. You have much to look forward to in the coming year. At last the hoopla over the election will end and the news will return to some semblance of watch ability. Of course if the far left is correct and we don't change our ways they have scheduled the world to end in twelve years anyway.

In the meantime, God bless America and the elderly.

REASON

When I was a child I understood as a child, I thought as a child and now that I'm an old lady, I still do They say, and I often have to wonder who they are, by the time you arrive at the ripe old age of eight you have reached the age of REASON I always looked forward to having Mother's Oats in the morning for breakfast, even though now they (same people) call it Oatmeal in spite of the facts, it looks, smells, tastes. and satisfactorily fill you up as all comfort food does. it was UNREASINABLE to change that lovely name for something so generic. I still haven't gotten over my delight in diving into a peanut sundae, or licking a lolly pop. I must admit, however, Sundays have taken a turn for the worst because of the loss of Joe Palooka and Flash Gordon in the paper's comic section. While we're reminiscing about favorites, who could ever forget Tarzan's physic, as he flew through the Jungle with lucky Jane at this side, and the ever giggling Cheetah, not far behind. His yodel must have required a tremendous amount of lung capacity because the only other person in the world able to emanate the ape man, came along later, in the form of Carol Burnett.

Once the government slapped a two cent tax on top of the 25 cents we were already paying at the box office, it became a little weighty to attend a picture show, even if they were giving out dishes. My love for the Hollywood scene was so strong I took a job at a cinema and became an usherette. That's how I circumvented the IRS and am still trying to do so anyway I can which seems REASONABLE to me.. During my ushering days, I discovered, while waiting for your next customer with your back to the screen (mandatory,) if you placed your flashlight at just the exact position in line with your left eye, you could watch the show reflected in the lens of the of the flashlight and still retain your employment. I REASONED this all out by myself at about sixteen. So, along with the rest of America's women I became addicted to the s shenanigans of Tyron Powers, Errol Flynn, and the not much of a hunk, Humphrey Bogart. I now find myself stuck in this new era of grubby beards and too much cleavage, and not even having a clue as to knowing any of the so called stars of today I must assume they are one of the REASONS the great HOLLYWOOD sign., once it disintegrated,was never restored.

As to attire, if you are flamboyant at eight, you are most definitely are flamboyant by eighty.. Friends tell me I seem to have an over abundance of shoes and clothing..

All I know about that is this. If you hang around this planet long enough and not of a mind to dispose of still usable garments, it would seem REASONABLE to me that one would accumulate a more than adequate assortment of stuff. I think my family is concerned about how to get rid of all this junk, but I am confident they can handle any situation with aplomb. And "why not?" I ask myself. They are all like their mother REASONABLE

LOOKS

Since there is nothing to do these days, except to sit and stare at each other from your designated spaces, I have come to realize through my dining experiences (when our masks are lowered to half-staff,) what an amazing amount of different looks there are in one small room. First there is that disgruntled look, (scowl) The disrespectful look, this surly one, the unhappy or sad one, and lastly there is the suspicious look This is exclusive among those of us who wish for our own food taster. or for those who have already tasted. Even more amazing is how's many different directions eyebrows can take in order to punctuate feelings. The furrowed brow sets the facial background for all feelings, including pleasantness. This consignment, (or however you wish to refer to it), were all going through is beginning to get on my one nerve, and I've spent many an hour contemplating actions I should take for my own amusement, especially now that you don't need bail money You can never depend on your kids for things like that. Besides they wouldn't dare incarcerate a woman of my age for fear of having "old lives matter." splattered all over East Bay Dr. In many ways our inability to travel about possibly should be considered a blessing. We do not have to worry about protesters mobbing us, or having our beautiful bird statues or our building defaced, but, of course, should they consider any of the above remember the elderly are protected and in control of the most powerful weapon. Just start coughing. You know the old saying "someday you'll look back and laugh at this." I don't think there's anything funny happening in our beloved country since China pulled the plug on us. So now it's up to us to not waste our limited time left wishing for things to be different. Let's make the most of what we have, like our families who we can Skype, or good health, considering all things, a great place to live, with people who care for us and most of all, each other. Just remember a look is worth 1000 words. I know, I know, it's a picture, but a look is a better fit for this situation. Keep smiling and enjoy.

FACES

I have been entertaining the thought of writing about noses just because there are so many different kinds of snouts among us. My favorite one is the Roman proboscis which is very straight, with a soft curving tip at the end.. The turned up and pugs are the cutest while the aristocratic schnozzles speaks for themselves. For your edification, I must add that fleshy noses are the most common. However since we really can't do any comparing, as to who has what because we all look like Billy the Kid during these masked days, we will subject ourselves to discussing the next feature,. our glorious lips.

I don't like the way today's young girls pump up their mouths until they look like an African Ubangi . Full lips are sensuous, it is true, but overfull are downright coyote ugly. Speaking of which, have you ever noticed how many women have all those little ugly lines around their mouths. I often wonder if it comes from petulance, since I've recently noticed the development of a few under my own nose. As for most men their look of their mouth is totally dependent on what they have surrounded it with. A mustache like Tom Selleck's is a woman's dream muzzle, but unkempt beards or grunge can be a big. turnoff Oh well, just another thing that no longer can be seen.

Let's spend some quality time thinking about the eyes. The windows to the soul. These orifices are usually the most striking and beautiful part of our faces, and the the lamps of our bodies. Just the variance of colors is like a phenomenon in itself. Did you know that when you were born your eyes were as big as they ever will get, but your beaks and ears continue to growth for as long as you live. I check the growth of my oracles on a daily basis because I think the elastic in these masks make them stick out sufficiently to, give me a look reminiscent of Dumbo.

The one positive thing to come out of mask wearing is that we can all imagine that behind those uncomfortable, optical smudging, unbearably hot pieces of cloth, hides a smile of appreciation for having being taken care of by people who truly care and all is well, as usual, in our homes, the beautiful Royal Palms.

FAMILIES

All articles concerning pain in humans decry the fact men's threshold for pain is exceedingly higher than that of women. I've also read if it became mans duty to bear children, we would follow the lead of the Chinese, and become a one child per family society. I must agree with these opinions if only from personal experiences and observations. When a male suffers with the flu, a cold, or any minor ailment, the attentive female constantly questions as to his needs to say nothing of his comfort, as she checks to see if he has a temperature. When and if the situation reverses itself, the only thing a man does is walk to the ailing wife's bedroom door to ask "What's for dinner?" Men may deny this, but women will verify it as a truism. These typical types of actions can only be attributed to excessive coddling by the mother of the family. Any male, fortunate to have older female siblings surely remember how big sister brought them their glass of milk at the start of dinner, wiped their grimy little lips during dinner, and then marched off to do the dishes after dinner. I think mothers have a tendency to dote on male children because their husband is so ecstatic over having a son, some of his exuberance rubs off on her. This, then, results in the husband having to share in mom's devotion as it passes from father to son. which, in turn, becomes the beginning of the training of yet another inept husband. The one thing mom should instruct their son about is, never looking wistfully into space as he uttering, "It's good, but not like my mom used to make." I believe in some states that's grounds for divorce.

On the other side of the coin, many a female child turned into daddy's little girl, and is pampered all her life by a man who could find no wrong in her, no matter how vile the act her mother complained to him about. These usually were the girls who had Shirley Temple's dimples, natural curly hair, and loved sitting on daddy's knee while she curled his hair around her little finger. She was sure to get a car for graduation, had only one child so daddy could be grand daddy, and wadded through several marriages as she searched for the man who would treat her just like you know who.

All parents have a favorite child, even though they would never admit to it, and especially not to the other children. As for the kids, they are always accusing you of favoritism even when they are the favorite and know it. There are a number of reason for this preferential parenting and most revolve around you. the parent. Should a poor child, having struggled through the throws of wriggling its way into this word, was unfortunate enough to be a mirror image of one of it's life givers, the poor thing is subjected to head patting and peacock strutting each time the subject of how much they resemble their parent is broached by an observer. To follow in the footsteps of one parent, by choosing a sport or career in which one parent excelled in, presents that parent with another chance to relive their life through the poor kid and correct all the mistakes committed by them.. The favorite comment becomes, "I know what's best for you, I've been there" Or "Give me the run down on your day." The experienced parent turns into the nosy nagger, and the child prays for temporary deafness each time it hears, "I just have to tell you something it will only take a minute."

Regardless of the horrific teens, the choosing of not quite acceptable spouses, the days of experimenting with drugs and booze use, most families end up still loving and respecting their members. and all go together to Grand ma's for Thanksgiving Dinner. It's the American way.

LIFE STORIES

How many times have you bashed this side of your head with your open palm while muttering," oy vey, I should have written a book ." With the exception a very few, most of us will lead lives of highs and lows, ups and downs, misery and happiness, preordained for us by the circumstances of our+ entrance into this world. If you were born gagging on a silver spoon you already know what is expected of you, and your destiny has already been decided. You will succeed in everything you do, go to Harvard, and marry into a wealthy family, or snag a baron and become a socialite during which time all will join in becoming one of the good old boys club. As for the remainder of us gagging down our first bottle, while whining to be breast-fed, nothing has been pre planned for for us. We were totally free to follow our parents lead or create something new, like the flower children did in the 60s. Almost all of us were bullied in school and chastised by teachers and parents while we muddled through our teens, consumed with worry about our looks, getting a boy or girl friend, or just having a friend. We didn't sweat the small stuff like good grades or the usual moms threats,"Just wait till your father gets home." It's all just a part of growing up without responsibility. Now comes the important part, making decisions about whether to go to college, go to work, or get just get married and go to work.

Which introduces us to the second chapter of our lives, the arrival of planned or unplanned children, mother-in-law's, money problems, and the responsibility of raising a family You take them all to Disney World, where the principle finds you to report one of your kids has flunked third grade. You get a raise, your partner loses their job. You buy a new house, oil prices soar. You and special friends plan a cruse. A loved one dies. You get a promotion and begin to feel successful, your daughter leaves her husband and moves home with three small kids.

Chapter 3, the children are finally gone, empty nest syndrome sets in.. Philandering husband, faithless wife. You think about retiring, the market plunges Your golf game is not what it used to be, your partner is getting fat. Your drinking too much, your partner joins you.

By the time you've made your final arrangements, you look back and say it could've been worse, just look at what happened to Jack and Jill or Dick and Jane. Your thoughts comfort you. You look at your partner and wonder how the both of you have managed being together all this time without having committed some kind of mayhem or murder. You look wistfully at each other and notice some new gray hairs, a few more wrinkles around the eyes, but grateful to have made it through life together, despite all the set backs Leaning back in your recliner, you begin to reminisce and truly begin to wonder if you may have a best seller on your hands.

THE DOCTOR VISIT

If, by some stroke of bad luck, you find yourself scheduled for a doctors visit, be prepared to devote almost an entire day to it, The waiting time alone is rarely ever under an hour. Leave us not forget the hours spent in preparation. The showering, pampering the choosing of the correct apparel We definitely do not want to be caught with our pants down, or some other similar facsimile while in the doctor's office When finally we are privileged to enter into the doctors den, we smile in gratitude, anticipating his undivided attention, while he, wearing the snow white jacket that causes syndrome in some people, peers intently into his computer in an effort to remember why you're here again. Once he makes his discovery, he performs a cursory examination taking your blood pressure and listening to your heart, ling and aah sounds. Needless to say these actions take place on the outside of all the layers of clothing you were so fastidi0ous about. After pushing his glasses back up his nose, and emitting a few mysterious sounds, he flashes his best bedside style smile in your direction, and either writes a prescription or announces your e good for another hundred thousand miles, or at least till you see him again in three months. You have spent a total of twelve minutes in the sanctuary. Now comes the time consuming part. For the gal at the desk, checking out patients must necessitate an abundance of patience on her part. Just finding a time comparable to both parties always seems to touch off some kind of query that causes knotted eyebrows and frustrated sighs. Unfortunately for her, this is only the beginning of her obligation to the patient. Further duties call for the writing of the reminder card, and the figuring out and collection of the co-pay.

Why is it, these receptionists always wear the faces of reluctant bank tellers if they are obliged to make change? We, the patient, arrive home with the need for an afternoon nap and waste no more precious time getting in our kip, Because of our ever present need to compare, let us take a look back on the old doc who still made house calls, delivered your children, and knew every one of their names. He wasn't a left or a right nostril specialist. His specialty was medicine, and his knowledge of all of it made him a master of diagnostics. A visit to the doctor then found you hardly in the door before the man himself was there to greet you with rolled up sleeves and a welcome smile. After a short discussion concerning the family, he got down to business, and listened intently while you rattled off your ailments. Sometimes it was necessary for him to consult a text book, but most often than not, after a bit of pondering, he would go into another room and return with all the medicine it would take to make you well again. You then ponied up two dollars, and if you were lucky enough to have a five, he would stuff it in his pocket and come up with the change from a pocket on the other side of his pants. Shaking hands and walking you to the door was the norm, as he suggested you call him when you need to see him again. I know we've come a long way, baby, but was it in the right direction? I think Modern Medicine redeems itself by helping us to live longer and more productive lives, despite the many, many restrictions and rules forced upon them by health care system and our ever present Government God bless to days practitioners who do no harm.

SONGS FROM THE SIXTIES

When I was a young girl I had three great friends. SWEET CAROLINE. RUN AROUND SUE, and PROUD MARY. Each, very different, but all very dear, Caroline was an innocent, sweet girl who loved SITTING ON THE DOCK OF THE BAY, watching the MOON GLOW, and singing quietly to herself, WHAT A WONDERFUL WORLD. Then reaffirming with I SAY A LITTLE PRAYER, because I'M A BELIEVER, and I believe in LOVE AND MARRIAGE, and some day, WITH THE HELP OF A FEW FRIENDS, MY PRINCE WILL COME, and I'll be taking THAT MAGIC CARPET RIDE Now Mary being quite the opposite, insisted, everyone STAND BY ME because THERE AIN'T NO MOUNTAIN HIGH ENOUGH, which she couldn't climb or nothing she couldn't do. Mary, of course, being from from NEW YORK, NEW YORK, had a very SUSPICIOUS MIN and the bad habit of regarding everyone as a CHAIN OF FOOLS. She expected attention EIGHT DAYS A WEEK so I was most surprised and happy to hear through the grapevine, that AT LAST, she had found someone DOWN ON THE CORRER that she was Crazy about, and eventually had to admit to being NOT TOO PROUD TO BEG, telling him " BABY I NEED YOUR LOVE," and they ended up being HAPPY TOGETHER. Now Sue was a CALFORNIA GIRL an felt It was NOT UNUSUAL no matter what she did or said. She would whine, I CAN'T HELP MYSELF Just CAN'T HELP FALLING IN LOVE Guys just FLY ME TO THE MOON she'd holler, then, turn into A RING OF FIRE, as she performed THE TWIST AND SHOUT. I agreed with her, but advised all she really needed was to stop being a HONKY TONK WOMAN and find just one right man because WHEN A MAN LOVES A WOMAN and tells her, YOU'RE ALL I NEED she usually finds herself responding to him with, HOW GREAT IT IS TO BE LOVED BY YOU. When She found me to be correct her only awe fulled reply was AIN'T THAT A KICK IN THE HEAD?

THE BODY

If you can recall we recently discussed the eyes, nose, lips, an hairs on our heads, so I thought it might be fun to drop down to our magnificent torsos, and examine them from neck to knees. Before we begin, I will confess to being somewhat biased on this subject. I always wondered if God only had the propagation of the race on his mind when he created Adam, but diversified his thinking when working on Adams rib. Of course there are all those rippling muscles to be considered, if you are into that kind of thing. but then there's also all that scratching. A woman's body is not only beautiful, but filled with purpose They can suckle, give birth, and pleasure men, but do have the need to be adorned with more than one fig lea. That fact, alone covers the necessity for most of them to maintain an expansive wardrobe. Having made that statement, let us discuss it in greater detail, starting below the neck. I start there only because there is nothing to be said for a mans neck, except it has a need to be shaved, while a woman's is said to be swan like. A woman breasts are a study in the exquisite, proven by the number of artists who have labored over the task of painting them. A mans chest is hairy. A woman's mid section displays a small sensual bump, right below her navel. A males belly is totally dependent on the size if his diners or the amount of beer he consumes. When it comes to butts, I will have to admit, men run a very close second, and garner much attention. I also concede that thighs can be a problem for some women, but then again, men's thighs are just hairy. Women are graceful, and light on their feet. Men are, oh well, we've all seen them lumbering by. In conclusion, (do I hear applause from the male side?) let's just conclude. and agree, that whatever the difference between us humans, we most definitely are attracted to one another and love is a beautiful thing.

NOTHING

I was coming up with nothing new to write about, so I decided to write about NOTHING If you think back a few years ago Jerry Seinfeld's series about NOTHING became a viable contender for first place TV fodder, so it would seem there is much to be said about NOTHING. For example if you tell yourself, "I am going to do NOTHING to day." it, of course, would be a fallacy, unless you are planning to go to your great reward. If not it is necessary to breath, to eat, to care for your bodily functions, which at times, can be a great deal of SOMETHING. To make and take phone calls, take your pills, brush your teeth etc, etc. In a similar pattern, it is totally impossible for your mind to do NOTHING. Example: If you were to light a candle in a darkened room and stare at it relentlessly for a one minute period, you could close your eyes and retain the image of the candle, which will last less than a minute, because your mind will automatically focus on something else. Think again about the flame and it will appear again for a short while. You can continue this futility until the mind exert a mind of its own, and the flame disappears. When you find yourself with NOTHING to do, try this, especially if you are a control freak.

Let us return to the over used NOTHING word, "There's NOTHING in there." a man will say as he points to his son's head.. How about the statement "There's nothing I wouldn't do for you." Usually uttered by men wanting something done for them. When a resolute individual strongly avers," I feel absolutely NOTHING concerning that situation," The caution light begins flashing regarding the veracity of that declaration. "There is NOTHIG more to be gained." A proclamation of defeat There's NOTHING I wouldn't give if I could just change it." Wishful thinking. "He was a good for NOTHING" Insult. "It turned out to be NOTHING after all." A relief comment. I now find myself in the dilemma of having NOTHING more to say.

ELEVATORS

I have been cogitating lately on how different the world would be today if Elisha Graves Otis had not perfected the elevator in 1859., one hundred and sixty years ago. The first skyscraper rose from the dust in Chicago in 1885. This indicates to me, it must have been a very short drop during those 28 years, since what was considered a skyscraper then, was only ten stories high. The other side of the coin is, (think about it,) how could we ever get from the ground floor to the fifth without Ole Otis. I'm sure that is the reason the the powers that be at the Palms, realizing what a hardship that would present, allow us to waddle around in the stair well during a fire drill. Like every thing else in life, there are pros and cons concerning the viability of every situation. For example, what about those of us who are claustrophobic, and stand holding our breath during our flight, swearing to ourselves we will walk back down if the elevator Gods will deliver us safely this time. Of course the pandemic has sort of put a damper on the crowding state of affairs. Now we only have to deal with how much after shave or perfume our six foot away companion has decided was sufficient that day. One more con concerning our lifts, you had better hightail it out of there if you don't want to lose some of your tail feathers during your exit. The doors seem to have a mind of their own. Have you ever noticed how the cage, when starting out in either direction, emits a small sound of effort and sometimes shudders just enough to make us do the same. This is particularly frightening when you are riding one of those that hang on the outside of a building. I am convinced Otis had a morbid sense of humor to allow for his pulleys and cables to emanate all these scary sounds. Today only about 26 people a year die due to elevator accidents, and most of those are technicians working on them. I must admit I'm a white knuckled plane flier and get the same unwelcome sensations when entering the hoist, so pay no attention to me, and continue to enjoy your ups and downs

THE STORY OF HAIR

Although we have already discussed the many aspects of our features we have, wrongly omitted analyzing the importance of our hair, how we got it, and how it has affected our lives. For a woman it is the essence of her crowning glory. For a man it becomes a travesty as he loses it. I would like, at this point, to interject some pertinent information for your edification. I should say education.. I'll bet you never imagined, or even thought about the fact that we have exactly the same number of follicles as a primate, and yet we are the only animal on this planet subjected to baldness.. Have you ever wondered why and when we all became less hairy? Evolutionists opinions differ, but I, personally consider Darwin's explanation most noteworthy. His thinking is that by the time we were standing upright, (seven million years ago) we were inhabiting the Savannah, and had to shed some fur in order to withstand the tremendous heat. He also believed the evolution fairy allowed, (for (our own good, of course) the retention of some hair in strategic places . The head was most certainly on that list, it's mission, to initiate more attractive humans which would then begin to produce a more appealing race. It always,somehow goes back to that apple.

My thoughts are straying so we best get back to hair. There are so many kinds of it, curly, kinky, straight, stringy thick, thin, frizzy, or just plain unmanageable. It really doesn't matter because we all don,t want to be without it Then there is the color to be considered. A quick trip to the salon, in one afternoon, can completely transform your appearance, no matter what the chimps had in mind for you. A fiery redhead, a saucy brunette, or a dumb blond. No matter what, hair is most definitely an asset if properly groomed. As a last resort you can always rely on a wig or toupee. Sometimes looking better than you did without it. Your only problem then is the wind One last bit of info concerning our ancestors. Did you know that underneath all that fur the skin of a chimp is as white as ours.?

The thought sort of makes me want to scratch something.

NANA

I have two grand daughters who arc enthralled with the forties. The music, the war, the Joan Crawford hairdos, the entire goings on with the greatest generation. One is a geriatric physician, taking care of the elderly, while the other can sit for hours and listen to my lies. Perhaps I shouldn't say exactly lies, but in your hearts you know all grandparents have a tenancy to exaggerate when they look back, or should I say not quite remember things the way they truly were in order to remain impressive. Perhaps fabricate would be a better choice. All our sacrifices like butter, sugar, meat and gasoline were consider small potatoes back then, because we had a cause and the will to preserve our way of life. It was Tom Brokaw, years later, who made hero's out of us, which we gratefully accepted and loved to expand upon, about the length of our suffering, and the depth of our patriotism. We also had the Big Band Sound and the voices of Bing Crosby and Perry Como to brighten up our lives. but fail to mention them. preferring to remain martyrs to the end. I must admit to days music makes me cranky and is an affront to my hearing. Lucky for me, my earlobes are long enough to fold over and stuff into my ear canal in place of ear plugs. Also, getting up before ten in the morning is enough to curl my hair, and succumbing to all of these delightful desserts at the Palms is a weakness in myself that I find, not only deplorable, but fattening. Of course, in the interest of maintaining my esteem, as matriarch of the family, I keep these fallacies to myself. The face presented to the new kids on the block is always kind, smiling, and covered with wrinkle hiding make up. Most people would consider this vain, but to me it's a matter of self preservation. I would like to be remembered, not for the person I really am, but as that feisty old lady we had so much fun with.

OUR WONDERFUL WORLD

Did you ever take a moment to wonder how the world turns on it's axis, and how it impacts yours? All the great minds, including Einstein, that pondered this subject ended up with an atomic bomb on their hands, so we will only investigate how the spinning of every known planets, in the universe spinning in the same direction, (counter clock wise,) affects our lives. First, the moon has it's own gravity pull,which creates the tides. When the moon is full and the tides are high some people have a tenancy to turn into werewolves, or simply go mad. As a matter of fact, studies show suicides, births, deaths and violence rise during this lunar phase . I'm sure most of you have heard the expression "it must be full moon". The more engrossing affect of full moon is romance. What man or woman could truly say they haven't, when cuddling with their significant other, been influenced by that mesmerizing golden glob in the sky, knowing full well the man in the moon condones all lovers and their actions while under his spell.. This point is so interesting because men are usually so blaze in the romantic category when they are not needy, while women are dependent on romance and being fawned over. It's all a part of being a female.

Earth's weather has a profound influence over humans and their well being. The production of edible food, the clothes they wear, the severity of pain from arthritis and, of course, that all important sperm count. Some of the above are reasons people over 70 move to Florida. Weather also impacts our moods. Sad is a depressive disorder, transforming people in the fall and winter. (Why we live in Florida.) A study showed a lot of rain can cause aggression in some people. (Why we live at the Palms.) You all know, of course, the world is on a wobbly tilt, and all of us tilt right along with it because of gravity. That word, gravity has reduced all our body parts to sagging like a weeping willows. I am deeply indebted to whomever invented bras. I don't know what to suggest to you guys whose waistlines have sunken to your thighs. Perhaps suspenders. I regress. Getting back to our tilting world, I truly believe it should be held responsible for some of the strange ans and improbable things performed by humans as they age. Walking at a tilt your whole life would, I suspect, have some ramifications on the gray matter. in some way. That's my excuse, and I"m sticking to it.

WHAT'S GOOD FOR YOU

From the cradle to the grave we are constantly told by family, friends, teachers, and physicians, what is good for us. Let's start with mother's milk which supposedly gives us a mush better start in life than the lowly man-made formula. During our first year we are forced to gag down many poor tasting vegetables, including strained spinach. I blame that on Popeye We teethed on Schweibock, a tasteless piece of hard toast, which forced our teeth to break through our gums. No wonder we were all cranky during this period. Please keep in mind that during the first three months of your entrance into this valley of tears the CDC (Center for Disease Control and Prevention) dictates that you should receive vaccines for hepatitis, diphtheria, whopping cough, etc., etc. It's an amazement to me that during this period babies begin to smile and coo, By age 2 pediatricians will insist on vaccination for influenza. Please keep in mind that all of this is and was good for you. During your teens and college years the medical profession came up with a meningitis vaccine to protect not only you, but your roomy, as well. For some reason even I can not explain, the word protect reminds me of the fact that condoms were invented by Charles Goodyear in the year,1839. Oh well, this vaccine stuff continues all through your lifetime. Even now, we are under the thumb of the AMA, as we subject ourselves to the never ending flu shots the pneumonia shots, the shingles shots, etc., etc. As I write this I'm straining to remind myself, all of this is good for me. I guess I'll just have to content myself and accept the wisdom of the FDA as they recall the drug I've been taking for the last ten years

I'd like now to discuss food. Sometime during the 80s eggs were pronounced evil, and blamed for creating high levels of cholesterol and heart disease. After a few years of reconsideration eggs were forgiven, and said to be a great source of protein, and a healthy non saturated fat. Ditto for butter and oleo, potatoes, dairy products, and raw nuts. Again I'll have to depend on the FDA mind changes for guidance.

Let us examine the best drinks. Pomegranate juice, green tea, cranberry juice, lemon water, and orange juice, are among the healthiest. I think for this category a Tanquera gin martini and olives stuffed with blue cheese as a garnish, tops the taste list and greatly improves your person ability which, in turn, has a direct affect on your health, ergo...IT'S GOOD FOR YOU no matter what the FDA says.

MODERN DAY NURSERY RHYME

There was a little girl who had a little curl
Right in the middle of her forehead,
And when she was good, she was very very good
But when she was bad she was torrid.
So Jack was tempted soon by Jill
To go with her right up that hill.
To have some fun, a little laughter.
Jack turned her down and went to town.
Thinking maybe she'd come after.
But she went to visit Mary's lamb,
Whose fleece was white as snow,
But every time that Jill was bad,
The lamb told Mary so
Rub a dub dub she found some guys in a tub,
And who do you think was there?
A butcher at Baker a candlestick maker,
They all made friends and went to the fair.
They soon found Jack Horner,
Right there in his corner,
Eating his favorite pie.
Taking one look at Jill he couldn't sit still
Shouting what a bad boy am I!
Now Jack could never eat no fat.
And Jill could eat no lean,
So they were married happily,
And licked their platters clean.

WEATHER

We've made it through the summer. the humidity, the heat
Knowing in our heart of hearts next year will just repeat.
Fall is near, but not yet cool, changing leaves not seen,
We sit here held a captivated in our world of ever green.
While we look about for something to replace what we will miss,
The wonders and the magic of the frost's first tender kiss.
Where trees create a canvas, as only they can do,
Russets, gold and orange, against a sky of blue
Of course we have our Palm trees. each with a different name
No matter how you cut it, somehow it's not the same
Next comes Old Man Winter, with those February rains,
But then again, without them, we'd have no reason to complain.
The weather is a subject we can not live without,
It governs us like day and night, of this there is no doubt.
Weather is our greatest theme and helps us to converse,
Without it we'd have naught to say, it rules our universe.
It saves us when a pregnant pause rears it's ugly head
We can always talk of weather or a book that we have read.
So whether you like it or whether you don't, weather is her to stay
Just force a smile, open that door and have a wonderful day.

LIES

To tell a lie is to take the path of least resistance. When in the middle of a confrontation it is sometimes easier to just to pretend your adversary has convinced you of his belief, rather than to continue to the hassle of debating something you know is positively correct. It becomes a lie of convenience, just like when you complement someone regarding their appearance, knowing full well they look like something the cat dragged in. This is deliberate deceitfulness, but still in the minor league of of venial sin. When we lied about stealing from her mother's purse, or other symbols or actions we moved up a notch to a moral, because tales with a purpose are the worst kind of lies, but the most profitable. Almost like a daily ritual, I would hear these words from my mother's lips, "Oh what tangled webs we weave, when first we practice to deceive." By the time I reached high school not lying had become a problem of better organization. Was it a little fib, a little white lie, a white lie, a big fib, or a whopper? By then I was desperate for different excuses not to see certain people, it still happens to me sometimes, which has transformed me into an accomplished liar. As all liars know it is something that can be destructive to relationships if you struggle with the remembering problem. It also helps develop a glib tongue and a quick mind in order to lie your way back out of it. We are all born liars, the first thing to enter our virgin ears is how babies are delivered by Mr. Stork, complete with pictures. Then came Jolly old Santa, the Easter Bunny, the tooth fairy, and the most disturbing of all the bogeyman. I don't now how parents managed to keep a straight face when they chastise their children in regard to lies. We can all turn over a new leaf and make a concentrated effort to be honest Abe's. However we must consider all the fun we would denying ourselves. Sometimes it is more than pleasurable to bamboozle one of your very best friends with a little white lie, and that's the truth.

BOOKS

Just try to imagine what this world would be like without the pleasure of reading a book. From the days of the caveman, the urgent need to make a statement was so strong they utilized their arduously honed hunting stone to carve out a message on the walls of their caves. Here's a fact that's hard to swallow. The first language sounded like Yoda. That little green Jedi from Star Wars Later the Egyptians used reed brushes and created a formal writing system that included 1,000 distinct characters, each with their own meaning. Cursive hieroglyphs were used on papyri paper. (listen up, teachers of today.) I bet you don't know who wrote the first true length novel. Fifth four chapters is a clue. It was a woman, of course. I don't think men had that much to say in the 11th century, or even since. Women, on the other hand, , have been blessed with the ability, in the 11th century, and ever since to transfer their bodies into vessels of endless chatter. It is truly an amazement for me to discover there are, presently, more male than female authors.

Today there are all kinds of publications. Books for dummies, how to books for the helpless, Roget Thesaurus for the language impaired, gardening books,cooking books,, how to improve your golf score, your tennis game. Talking about improvement, from 1980 to 1990 we could read or listen to the radio and hear Dr Ruth discuss sex, where we could learn all the things our parents failed to tell us. Let us not forget Dr. Masters and Virginia Johnson who took it a step further. What about all those historic novels describing the mischief that went on in the courts of England. Those people made their own history! Then we have the mighty mystery, designed to scare the pants off of you while you are trying to pinpoint the guilty party before the detective does. Travel books are good, but actual travel is beret. Sometimes I feel like a space cadet but not enough of one to enjoy those missiles on the galaxy and all those strange beings supposedly out there. They are just not my brand of martini. There are millions of books on the planet so those crazy protesters can have a field day trying to burn them all, but there will always be books. The only kind of publication I don't care for is an autobiography. First of all it takes a tremendous amount of vanity to write about yourself and think there is someone out there that really gives a fig. If the person is very famous it's a book of vindication anyway. We already know the truth from the tabloids and the author is trying to talk us out of it.

I will close with something profound and true. Of all the million and million of bound literature available to us, the Bible is still the best seller.

HOW SWEET THE SMELL OF SUCCESS

I have always wanted to become a published author, and finally at the age of 86 was successful with my book about the anthracite coal miners. The book is called Miner's Haven and depicts the hardships and despair suffered by the miners under the rule of the miners owners and the union. I would like to quote one of the miners sayings which they used to keep body and soul together.

"Things turned out best for those who make the best of how things turn out."

It takes grit and perseverance to get what you want in this life, and it's never too late to get started. Quitting is never an option. Best of luck to all you wannabes out there. **Never give up!**

Author ELAINE SHARShON

Printed in the United States
By Bookmasters